REVIEWS

'Finally, a helpful and refreshingly objective book on the subject: you can count on Mark's integrity and insight into the market to give unbiased and crucial advice for those who need it most. Very easy to read and stuffed full of real-life examples, this book cannot fail to give candidates the best chance to succeed in the most competitive of markets. A must have for candidates who want to improve their performance.'

- Alexandra Cooper, Founder at Cooper Edwards

'A very practical and easy to read book with lots of real life tips and strategies. Having recruited candidates across many functions, nationalities and countries the tactics in this book will cut across all of these areas. If candidates were to engage in the tools, techniques and tips outlined within this book they would be in the best position to gain their next and desired, role.'

- David Steel, Executive Coach at Interserve Learning & Employment International

'This book contains many great tips on how to prepare for an interview. If you are looking for a professional, practical and comprehensive guideline of how to successfully pass a job interview and get the job you want – you must read this book. Mark James Walsh has managed to identify and understand what winning candidates do to swing the final decision in their favour and he presents it in a way that everyone can put into action. All you need to do is read this book and follow the "Top Preparation Tips" to get the job you want.'

- Sharon Ron, CEO at HRSR

REVIEWS

'The essential guide on how to succeed at interview. Refreshingly corporate jargon free. 'The Seven Deadly Sins' hits the nail on the head with where you need to be psychologically and where you need to put the hiring manager psychologically and everything in between to secure that dream opportunity.'

- Kieran Hinphey, Director at Reach Personnel International Ltd

'As a recruitment consultant with over 25 years' experience in the industry, I can thoroughly recommend Mark's book. It provides easy to use tips that will increase your chances of success in any recruitment process, whatever your level of work experience. It effectively puts you on the other side of the table, enlightening you to what the interviewer might be thinking. As Mark says, the best candidate does not always get the best job, but this book will help you be that best candidate.'

- Patrick Smith, Managing Director Northeast at Broster Buchanan

'An easy to read and practical guide on how to increase your chances of success in job interviews.'

- Andrew Mears, Director at Solutions Recruitment Group

The Seven Deadly Sins of Job Interviews

Mark James Walsh

LIMIT OF LIABILITY / DISCLAIMER OF WARRANTY

AUTHOR PROFILE

Mark James Walsh is an accomplished hiring professional with over fifteen years' experience implementing effective hiring strategies with international firms. He is a CMI Chartered Manager, holds a BSc (honours) and post graduate qualifications in project management, leadership and business administration

Mark's practical interview advice is based on insights gained from working right alongside hiring managers during thousands of job interviews. He has directly observed how successful candidates convince hiring managers to choose them ahead of the competition. He clearly explains how anyone can use these winning methods to achieve their best possible interview performance.

The "Seven Deadly Sins Of Job Interviews" captures the essence of what makes hiring managers decide to hire certain candidates. It uncovers the common pitfalls that cause hiring managers to reject candidates and explains how you can avoid them. This book will help you to learn from thousands of successful candidates who have already found their dream job.

MARK JAMES WALSH

CONTENTS

INTRODUCTION

Job interviews are hard to get. Current statistics show that only between two and five out of every one hundred job applications actually results in a job interview. The odds are even longer if you are applying to a market leading brand name business.

It is vital that you make the most of every job interview that you get.

The best candidate doesn't always get the job ………..

Being the best candidate does not guarantee that you will get the job offer. The impression that you make on the hiring manager has the biggest influence on the outcome of the interview. Inspiring confidence in the decision maker is absolutely crucial. The interview process favours confident, outgoing candidates who make a positive first impression. Confident candidates easily build rapport with the interviewer and do a really good job of promoting themselves.

Confident, extroverted and self-promoting candidates are often the most successful, but **you don't need these traits to guarantee success**. You can learn from winning candidates and replicate what they do to improve your chances of landing that dream job.

> **With the right preparation and practice, anybody can improve their job interview performance**.

It's all about convincing the hiring manager ......

In this book, I will explain how winning candidates use certain techniques to persuade hiring managers to offer them a job. I explore how they avoid the common interview pitfalls. I explain how they manage to inspire confidence with every answer. We will look at how they convince the hiring manager that they will solve their problems. The goal of this book is to identify these successful strategies and show you how you can use them to your advantage.

Throughout my HR career, I've participated in thousands of job interviews. I've studied the reactions of decision makers to the answers given by candidates. The more interviews I participated in, the more curious I became to understand the reasons why winning candidates are so much better. How do they manage to be so influential?

It's a decision-making process......

The purpose of a job interview is to allow the hiring manager to decide who is the best candidate for the job. Most people, hiring managers included, are not that good at making decisions. The job interview process is far from perfect. In fact, it is quite flawed and can be very subjective. The decision is often swayed by whatever bias or preconceptions the hiring manager has.

The interviewer doesn't know you but still has to form an opinion of your suitability for the job. They must make a decision in a limited period of time. The opinion they form is the main piece of information that they have to go on. This is almost entirely based on the impression that you create for them during the interview.

Your job is to make sure everything that you say and do creates a positive impression.

Lots of very capable and competent people are actually very poor at job interviews. The reason is that they have little or no understanding of what the hiring manager actually needs. To perform at your best, you must avoid anything that will create doubt or fear in the decision makers mind. Winning candidates manage the hiring managers fear. They make sure that every answer creates a positive impression.

Key Tactics and Techniques......

My experience, gained during thousands of job interviews, has allowed me to identify the key tactics and techniques that all successful candidates use. They say things in a way that appeals to hiring managers. They demonstrate specific attributes and attitudes that convince decision-makers to hire them. I have found these techniques to be remarkably consistent. They work across nationalities, genders, generations, sectors and industries.

Managing the fear....

Whenever any decision maker I was working with rejected a candidate, I asked for the reasons why. I worked hard to understand what caused them to reject the candidate. I found, in each case, that fear was the key factor. Fear that the candidate will not solve their problems. Fear that the candidate wouldn't be able to do the job, or that they wouldn't fit in with the existing team.

Keys to success.....

I also made sure to identify and understand what winning candidates do to swing the final decision in their favour. All successful candidates have the ability to inspire confidence and remove any fear that a hiring manager has.

Winning candidates make it very easy for the hiring manager to visualise them doing a good job.

Effective preparation
is essential ....

One of the key steps to achieving job interview success is effective preparation. In this book, I will show you how to ensure you have prepared yourself in the best possible way.

Knowing exactly how you will approach the interview will boost your confidence. It will improve your ability to handle tricky job interview questions.

Candidates who take this approach have much higher success rates in job interviews. I know because I've seen the evidence with my own eyes - **thousands of times**.

I will explain how you can take a planned approach to your preparation. You will learn how to focus on the job requirements, the hiring manager's needs and the culture of the organisation. This preparation will help you approach every question in a way that gives the decision maker what they need. You will learn how to inspire confidence and avoid any pitfalls. You will learn how to influence the decision-making process in your favour. You will dramatically improve your job interview performance.

--------- Thank you for buying this book. I hope you enjoy reading it and that you find it useful. If you do then, please leave a Five Star Amazon review ---------

SIN NUMBER ONE

Failing To Convince The Hiring Manager That You Can Do The Job

Can you actually do the job?

It sounds really obvious, but the first step in any job interview is showing that you can do the job. It's surprising how many people fail to convince the hiring manager that they can actually do the job. Many interviewers like to use a competency-based approach to assess applicants. This style of questioning asks you to share examples of how you used a particular competency or skill to do something.

The aim of this approach is to allow the interviewer to form a judgement of your skill level. Based on your responses the interviewer will form their judgement. This is usually based on some sort of rating scale. These scales normally have five levels ranging from basic knowledge, some knowledge or competence right up to highly skilled or expert level.

Your responses guide the interviewer towards giving you a specific rating for each required key skill or competency.

Key Competencies

To prepare for competency-based questions requires two things. First, you must study the job description and identify the key skills or competencies. Some businesses can overdo the specification and list dozens of requirements.

**You need to figure out which are the
most important skills for the job.**

The order in which they are written can be a clue. Often the most important are at the top of the list. I would always recommend that you focus on the most important four or five. Think of them as the basic skills necessary to do the job. Without them you would not be able to deliver what needs to be done in the role. Most hiring managers will be looking for a skill level somewhere between competent and expert level for their key requirements. Use the preparation checklist in Chapter Ten to note down the key skills required.

As an example, I recall getting feedback from a company Managing Director. Having interviewed an excellent candidate for a Sales Manager vacancy he decided not to hire the candidate. When discussing his thought process he explained that he really liked the candidate and felt he was very well prepared. He felt he knew the market really well and had a great understanding of the company's products. But, when it came down to his final decision he just wasn't convinced that the candidate had the necessary selling skills needed to be successful in the job. The candidate had ticked most of the boxes but he fell short in one key area and this meant he didn't get the job.

How do you rate?

Once you've identified the key competencies, **the second step is to assess where you fit on the scale for each one**. Now, this is where you need to be honest with yourself. This can be tricky to do. We all tend to have a biased view of our own ability. Most of us tend to over-estimate our ability to do something.

I've seen many candidates fail in interviews because they have clearly over-estimated their ability in certain areas. If in doubt ask some friends or colleagues for some feedback. Better still ask someone that you have worked for. Being able to show that "colleagues and supervisors tell me I'm a good organiser" shows evidence of your ability. Convincing evidence will inspire confidence in the decision makers mind. This type of evidence shows you have good open relationships with others because they're giving you feedback. Maybe you have received constructive feedback in the past telling you where you might improve in certain areas. This can be a good thing to share with an interviewer, especially if you can show that you've taken the feedback on board. Showing that you've recognised a gap and worked to increase your skill levels, by training or others means, will impress any interviewer.

How to be convincing

Give yourself an honest rating for each of the key required competencies. Think of two or three examples that clearly shows your skill level for each of these key requirements. There are many ways to show that you are skilled in certain areas:

- Being rewarded or acknowledged in some way for a job well done.
- People frequently asking for your help.
- Leaders showing appreciation for your work.
- Being asked to train other people in certain tasks.

These are all good signals and can be used to demonstrate your strengths to an interviewer. The best approach is to prepare some good examples that show how you've used a specific skill to solve a problem or deliver a benefit.

Top Preparation Tip:

> **Prepare some examples that demonstrate your ability for the key requirements of the job. Make sure you have evidence to support each one.**

Demonstrating expertise

If you are expert at something having evidence that clearly shows this helps to convince the interviewer. Being able to display an expert level of ability in any area means that you understand and can explain why the competency is so important to an organisation. This is a good way of demonstrating the high level of understanding that highly skilled people have. Explaining why you did things in a certain way gives a good impression that you really do know what you're doing.

For example, I watched a very talented software engineer answer each interview question by explaining why he had done things in a certain way to get the job done. The hiring manager told me that he felt the candidate was a real expert because he clearly understood there were a number of ways to address any problem. All of his answers showed that he had always chosen the correct approach at the right time for the right reasons, and he could explain why.

Keep it real

A candidate with an over inflated view of his or her abilities can be a very worrying prospect for any hiring manager. It creates trust issues and is a big alarm bell. If you don't have the required skill level don't pretend that you have! This is really off putting for a hiring manager.

My advice is to stick to the **key requirements** and convince the interviewer that you meet the required levels.

Shortcomings in skill level can be overcome with training and experience but you must first recognize where you fall short. Failing to recognise that you don't have the required skill level can be problematic and disruptive. You need to honestly assess your own skill levels against the key requirements. Few jobs require expert level knowledge in every area.

Convince the interviewer that you have the necessary skill level for the key requirements and you've made a very good start.

You don't need to know it all

Some of the required skills stated in the job description may not necessarily be essential. Organisations will often list dozens of required skills. Many may be just "nice to have" rather than being essential. There is a degree of judgement on your part as to which are essential and which are not. This can be difficult to get right, however, if in doubt you can always ask and seek clarification during the interview. Some requirements will be inherently obvious because of the nature of the job. You need to make sure you can demonstrate that you have the necessary skill level for these. Thinking about what needs to be delivered by the organisation and what the hiring manager needs will help you to decide .

If you do fall short in any specific area, then it is perfectly fine to admit this. Of course, you must also show that you understand where the gaps are and have a plan to show how you will address them. It's important to show that you will work hard to develop the specific skill. It's also important to show that you understand why it's required. Make it clear that you won't take unnecessary risks while you are getting yourself up the learning curve. Reassure the manager that you'll be happy asking for help and support as you learn your way into certain parts of the job. Don't ignore any gaps in skill level. They may come up for discussion during the interview so it's sensible to plan what you're going to say about them.

Top Preparation Tip:

> **Identify any skills gaps and add them to your preparation checklist. Be ready to acknowledge them and to talk about your plans to address these gaps.**

Gaps in your knowledge can actually be used as a selling point. You can explain why taking on a new role will give you an opportunity to learn and increase your skill levels. This can be presented as an excellent opportunity for you to further develop your career.

Remember that you are in a competitive situation

People often think of job interviews as a pass / fail exercise. Get through each question with an acceptable answer and you've passed the test; it's not that simple. It's very important to remember that you will be directly compared to other candidates. You will not necessarily be the best judge of how well your abilities and experience stack up against the competition. Your responses will be directly compared and judged against others. You may feel you're an expert in something, but there may well be someone else who is stronger than you.

Make your case and give the interviewer the opportunity to decide how they will judge your level of expertise. Don't assume that because you think you're an expert that the interviewer will agree with you. I've often seen hiring managers become quite irritated and even annoyed by candidates. The candidates were trying to pass themselves off as experts without having any evidence to support their claims. This never works and only results in a loss of trust and credibility.

Help the interviewer to form an accurate opinion

The interviewer needs to form a judgement about your skill levels and decide whether they exceed, meet or fall short of their needs. The main challenge in the early part of the interview is to create a positive impression and reassure the interviewer. For the first part of your interview, you need to help the hiring manager make that decision. This allows them to tick the box and move on to the next phases of the interview.

Top Preparation Tip:

> **Make sure you have some stories prepared that will demonstrate your key strengths and abilities. Add them to your preparation checklist and make sure each one is backed up with evidence.**

Using stories is an excellent way of demonstrating your key strengths. Everyone, especially hiring managers, like listening to real world examples. It's a great way to reinforce your point and people always tend to remember good stories. It's an excellent way of creating a strong positive impression with the hiring manager.

Being able to apply yourself in the new role

Having skill and ability is one thing. You need to be able to apply it in the right way for any given situation. Hiring managers often feel nervous about a candidate being able to apply themselves in their particular business culture or environment. If you don't make a good job of explaining how you will transfer your skills you won't be offered the job. Competency based questions give you an opportunity to give some strong relevant answers. Make sure that you have prepared some examples that show you can get the job done in the right way.

For example, an interviewer asks "have you ever had to deal with stock shortages before?". A good answer would be something like:

"yes, I have had to help resolve stock shortage situations in the past. I always made sure to inform our customers as soon as possible in the event of any problems."

An excellent answer will qualify this further saying something like:

> "shortages in that job were rare, but they caused a lot of problems when they did happen. We always made sure to have our couriers on standby to minimise any delay for the customer. We always kept the customer informed of exactly what was happening, what we were doing to fix the problem and when they would receive their order. We always followed up after the delivery had been made to make sure everything was OK and to apologise for the inconvenience."

This is a good example of an answer that shows you know how to deal with the issue, but it goes further than that. It shows you understand the impact on the business. It's always a good idea to sense check how your own experience will transfer into a new business environment.

A good way of doing this is to ask something like:

> "would you see any potential difficulties with me transferring my skills into your business?"

Top Preparation Tip:

> Make sure that your examples are relevant to the role and the organisation. Think about what the organisation does and what the hiring manager needs to deliver.

Soft Skills

Of course, technical skills or key competencies are only one part of the picture. Soft skills are also very important when it comes to working with other people. There's no point hiring a world expert in something if that person can't communicate and get along with others in the business. What are the key generic or soft skills that employers find most valuable?

Key Soft Skills

- Communication
- Leadership
- Problem Solving
- Flexibility
- Organising and planning
- Teamwork
- Interpersonal Skills

Hiring managers will always value team members that possess these types of soft skills. For example, I have heard many positive comments about candidates who have shown that they are strong communicators. This is because they are so much easier to work with. Hiring managers always value team members who are flexible. Being able to rely on someone who will happily do whatever needs to be done to solve a problem makes a hiring managers life so much easier. Helping out with planning and organising activities can be very beneficial to any manager. Prepare some examples that show you have these soft skills and that you can apply them. This will help you to build a positive impression.

These soft skills are always in demand with employers. **The ability to solve problems and get things done is highly valued.** They have a direct positive impact on the company's bottom line, and that appeals to all managers. Companies often boast about the attitudes of their employees and how they work hard for their customers. These attributes can be hard to teach and are often engrained into a person's character make up. You will often hear hiring managers talking about "attitude". All hiring managers will be keenly focused on discovering clues that demonstrate a candidate's attitude.

Winning candidates always demonstrate a positive, can-do attitude.

Application is crucial

Being technically gifted at something is all well and good. You also need to able to apply that ability at the right time and in the right place. Hiring managers see skills or competencies as important but that alone doesn't make you the winning candidate. At the end of the interview process, a decision must be made. The competency level is only part of that decision. Ultimately, the hiring manager is looking for somebody who will get the job done without any negative consequences. Having these key soft skills shows you're a team player, are good to work with and will be effective at getting the job done.

It's good practice to prepare some general examples that show your ability to use these key soft skills. Showing that you're a team player. Demonstrating how you're an effective listener and can solve problems really helps to reassure the interviewer. Some soft skills can be particularly valuable in certain situations. Communication skills can be very useful when working with remote teams. The ability to solve problems is very useful when working in organisations where there is little or no direct supervision of people's work. Always remember that you want the hiring manager to feel confident that you will solve their particular problems. Make sure that you also have some examples of soft skills that are particularly relevant to specific organisation you are interviewing with.

Top Preparation Tip:

- Certain soft skills, such as problem-solving, communication and team work are universally popular. Be ready with some examples to demonstrate your ability to use these skills.

- Other soft skills will have particular importance in certain roles and organisations. It's also worth preparing some examples which have specific relevance.

- Add these examples to your preparation checklist.

SUMMARY

- Identify the key competencies or skills required for the role.

- Complete an honest assessment of your skill level against each competence.

- Prepare some examples that will demonstrate your ability for each of the key requirements.

- Are you sure that you know why each skill is required in the job?

- Have you got some examples that demonstrate your relevant soft skills?

SIN NUMBER TWO

Giving The Impression That You Are Not Proactive And Can't Get Things Done

Managing people is not easy

Remember that the hiring manager you are being interviewed by is a line manager. That will most likely be their main responsibility on a day to day basis. This is an important point to keep in mind during your interview. Being a line manager is not an easy job. They must ensure that their team delivers results. They need to make sure each individual team member delivers what's required of them. They need to keep their team engaged and motivated and help them to develop their careers. They will need to plan for the future and make sure their team will meet the long-term business needs. That's a lot of things to juggle. For any line manager there is always a balance to be struck depending on the situation and the individual team members.

> **Key Fact**
>
> The only sustainable way to succeed as a manager is to hire and grow a team of capable and motivated employees.

All hiring managers are looking to recruit capable staff who will get the job done for them. The last thing that any hiring manager wants is to bring an under performer into their team.

Show you can get things done

As a job interview candidate, you must show that you can get things done. This always creates a positive impression in any job interview situation. All hiring managers gravitate towards those candidates that create the most positive impression. It really helps you to stand out if you can create this positive impression. The merest hint or suggestion that you don't like taking responsibility is very off-putting to any decision maker.

I saw a very clear example of the importance of showing you can get things done during an interview with a very experienced Engineering Manager. We were interviewing a young, highly qualified graduate for an entry level engineering role. The interview was going well until the Engineering Manager started to home in on a particular concern he had. I noticed that he kept probing the candidate on how he made sure his work was completed on time. What difficulties had he encountered and how had he overcome them? The candidate actually struggled to answer these questions. I discussed his feelings about the candidate straight after the interview. "I won't hire him because he clearly has difficulties in getting his work done on time. I need people who I can rely on to deliver." Unfortunately this young candidate had failed to inspire confidence in the hiring manager and didn't get the job.

Talking about your achievements and successes can help to create that positive impression. **It's very important to highlight your individual contribution.** Many people find this difficult and are uncomfortable doing so. It can feel like bragging and bragging feels unnatural to most of us. A good way to approach this issue is to identify the stories that showcase your strengths and abilities.

Top Preparation Tip:

Have some success stories ready to drop into the conversation. Add these examples to your preparation checklist.

Be crystal clear on what your contribution was and how that contributed to the final outcome. Think about what would have happened if you had not been involved. This can help you to show why your contribution was so important.

You may have used certain soft skills such as problem solving, creativity or strong communication skills. You can explain how this really helped to get everybody focused on what needed to be done, for example. Perhaps your input helped to solve a critical issue that nobody else had noticed. Your input had therefore directly resulted in a really positive outcome.

It's important to demonstrate your thought process in your answers. Showing that you did the right thing is good but it's not enough on its own. You must qualify it by explaining why you did what you did. Having the correct judgement to identify the problem and implement the right solution is a valuable skill to any business.

> **Key Fact**
>
> **Proactive doers are usually the most valued staff members in any organisation. They don't have to be asked twice to get things done.**

Proactive doers instinctively know what to do before being asked. Anticipating potential problems and identifying solutions is a valuable skill to have. All line managers put a high value on this ability and want it in their teams. People who bring them problems do not make a line managers life any easier.

Micromanagement

Being micromanaged is a widespread complaint. To be honest, I have never met a manager who enjoys having to micromanage their employees. This style of supervision invariably happens where there is a lack of trust. If a manager does not trust their staff to get the job done, then they feel obliged to micromanage the situation. Any suspicion that they will have to micromanage a candidate will discourage most decision makers from hiring that person.

Interview questions will often focus on what you do when you hit a problem or a road block. Think very carefully about using some examples that show how you figured out a way around the problem. Of course, you may not always have the perfect solution. Even so, it's very important to show that you can bring options and potential solutions to consider and discuss.

Problem Solving

You must demonstrate that you can solve problems, and not just because somebody told you to. Being able to find the root cause of any issues is very important. Examples that show how you identified a serious issue, understood the cause and found a solution work really well.

Make sure that your examples show how you identify problems or business needs and work to develop the right fix.

You should also show that you have the decision-making skills to prioritise what to work on. Winning candidates are always able to demonstrate this. They show how they make sure they're on track to do the right thing in line with business needs. A simple model which can help you is the STAR Model as outlined in Figure 1.

The STAR Model

SITUATION: Explain the context. What was the situation, outline the challenge, the circumstances and the difficulties you faced?

TASK: What did you need to achieve to solve the problem?

ACTIVITY: What did you actually do?

RESULT: What benefits resulted from your actions?

Figure 1

You can use the STAR model to demonstrate how you solved problems. The structured approach allows you to demonstrate your strength for particular competencies. An example might be a situation where a customer rings up to complain about a missing delivery:

Even though you're about to go to lunch, you explain to the customer that you're going to investigate the delivery details straight away and then call them back. You need to find out what the problem is and reassure the customer, fast. You manage to reach the delivery driver and discover there's been an accident on the route. He's diverted to another route and will be with the customer that afternoon.

You relay this to the customer who gets the delivery and is very pleased with the response to his complaint. The customer sends your boss a message praising your commitment and has remained a loyal customer ever since.

Show the benefits

Always make sure you explain why you did what you did when talking about how you can get things done. Make sure that you show how you took the initiative and planned what you were going to do. Don't forget to explain the results and benefits. Showing the impact on business performance is key to really sell the positive impact of your achievements.

We all make mistakes

Nobody is perfect and we all make mistakes from time to time. From the hiring managers perspective being able to deal with mistakes is very important. Self-awareness is crucial in showing that you have learned from previous mistakes. Making mistakes is fine as long as we learn from them. We all develop our decision making and problem-solving abilities as we increase our experience levels.

SUMMARY

- You must make it very clear to the hiring manager that you will solve their problems.

- Identify some key achievements and successes that show how your individual contribution made good things happen.

- Have some stories prepared that show that you can take the initiative.

- Make sure you have some examples that show you understand how to plan your efforts. You must show that you are good at prioritising what needs to be worked on and why.

- You must demonstrate that you can learn from your mistakes.

SIN NUMBER THREE

Failing To Make A
Lasting Positive Impression

The key barrier standing between you and your dream job is the hiring manager! In order to get that job offer, you must win them over. Every single thing that you say and do must create a positive impression for them. Successful candidates always manage to create a lasting positive impression and this helps them to stand out from the crowd. "I just never felt that the candidate had any enthusiasm for the role or our business." is feedback I've received many times from disappointed interviewers when they have rejected candidates.

Positive First Impressions

It's important to start the interview in a positive and enthusiastic way. You must demonstrate your enthusiasm for the role and the business right from the start. One great way to do this is to **make a good positive opening comment**. Something along the lines of the examples shown below shows your positive approach:

> "I'm delighted to be here today. I've read several recent articles about the impressive growth of the business, so I'm excited to learn more."

"Thanks for inviting me for an interview. I've known several people that have worked here over the years and I have always heard positive things about the business."

"I'm delighted to get the chance to meet with you. This is such an exciting industry and I'm very interested in learning more about your business."

"I was very pleased to be invited for an interview today. I heard about your expansion plans and the future looks really positive for the business."

Top Preparation Tip:

Make sure you have some positive comments ready to use at the start of the interview. Add them to your preparation checklist.

Preparing a positive opening line or comment helps to break the ice and get things off to a good start. Tell the interviewer why you're so interested in the job. If there is something about the company's mission or values that really appeals to you – make sure you point this out. Being up to speed with the latest company news helps to show you're on the ball. It also shows that you have researched the job and the company, helping you create a strong impression. If you can show how and why the role appeals to you, the impression you create will be even stronger.

> **Key Fact**
>
> **It's very common for interviewers to reject a candidate simply because they showed no enthusiasm. Never miss an opportunity to create a positive first impression.**

Showing up early, neatly presented, smiling when first meeting, having a firm handshake and being polite are very easy ways to help create a positive first impression.

Talk about the competition

Talking about the industry or sector can be a clever tactic. It shows you're focused in your job hunting approach and not just after any old job. This can often cause the hiring manager to feel that they don't want to lose you to a competitor. If they think you're a strong candidate then snapping you up you ahead of their competition makes them look good. It's certainly a good idea to mention that you are exploring options elsewhere within the industry. This appeals to the competitive nature of any hiring manager.

Let the interviewer manage the process

Once things get going, it's important that you allow the interviewer to work through the process. Some interviewers like to tell you about the business and explain what they're looking for. Others prefer to jump straight in and just start asking questions. Building rapport early on is important in delivering a good interview performance.

A key thing that you should try figure out is how much detail the interviewer likes to receive. Some people are very detail oriented and want to know exactly how and why you did what you did. Others are not interested at all in the details. They just want to hear about the benefits you can bring to their business.

Tailor your message
to suit the listener

Too much detail can bore some interviewers. Too little leaves others thinking you're not telling them the whole story. It's important to strike the right balance. Asking the interviewer some simple clarifying questions can help set you on the right track. It's a good idea to ask simple qualifying questions to make sure the interviewer is comfortable with your answers.

"Have I given you what you need?"

"Does that answer the question?"

"Have I explained things in enough detail?"

Don't unsettle the interviewer's natural style, if they want more detail give it to them. The questions that an interviewer asks you will give you a clue as to their preferences. Questions that drill down and look for more and more detail show you they want specifics. Some interviewers will only look for the bottom line result. They are not too interested in how you did what you did. They just want to know what you can do for them.

Top Interview Tip:

> You should always try and judge the interviewers response to your answers.

Ask questions but only at the right time

Don't overdo the questions in the early stages. Remember the interviewer must get through the basic decision points before the conversation can open up into a discussion. The typical hiring manager's thought process is outlined in Figure 2.

Job Interview Decision Making Process

Phase 1:   Can this person do the job to the required level?

Phase 2:   Will they fit in with the current team and the culture of the organisation?

Phase 3:   Will they be suitably challenged and engaged to stick around?

Figure 2

Always let the interviewer draw their own conclusions about your answers. Once you've given an answer, you need to observe the reaction of the interviewer. Don't presume they like the answer you've given. Let them be the judge of what you've said. Pay close attention to the interviewer's body language. Positive body language signs will encourage you to continue. Smiling or nodding in agreement suggests they like what you are saying. Frowning or facial expressions that show confusion means you need to stop and check if you're going off track.

Don't be afraid to stop and clarify what they're looking for in your answer. Pay particular attention to "interrupting" type questions. An interviewer may interrupt you or challenge what you say. These interruptions can be very telling. Make sure to pay careful attention and clarify anything that they may seem unsure about.

Do not ignore any signs that tell you that the interviewer is not happy with your answer.

Make sure you are focused on answering the question that has been asked. Always watch the response to your answer, if in doubt ask if they want more information. During an interview for a Quality Coordinator role the hiring manager had to repeatedly ask the same questions because he wasn't happy with the answers he was getting.

The candidate was trying to quickly move on from some topics as she couldn't provide a satisfactory answer. After the interview the hiring manager explained why he had to reject the candidate. She couldn't convince him that she had the level of knowledge required to do the job. He lost patience because she was rushing to provide an answer and move on to the next question. She seemed oblivious to the fact that she hadn't provided a satisfactory answer on several occasions.

> **Key Fact**
>
> **Not answering the actual question that's been asked always puts interviewers off.**

Some interviewers are open to you asking questions at any stage, others like to leave them until the end. It's a good idea to ask simple qualifying or clarifying questions throughout the interview. It's also fine to ask simple "sense checking" questions throughout. Broad or difficult questions that might put the interviewer on the spot are different. They are best saved until the end or until discussions have opened up a bit. Asking challenging questions can put the interviewer off and knock them off their stride. Remember you must let the interviewer get through the required steps of the interview.

Whilst being interviewed an experienced Project Manager suddenly stopped and said "It feels like I am talking a lot here, am I talking too much?". The hiring manager, a very experienced Operations Manager told her "keep going, you're doing a good job and you're answering a lot of my questions without me having to ask them". She got the job. She was a very good candidate and interviewed in a convincing manner. The fact that she stopped and looked for feedback to make sure she was on the right track impressed the interviewer. It helped to create the impression that she was a good person to work with.

Don't ask annoying questions

Asking inappropriate questions or asking questions at the wrong time can be very distracting for the interviewer. Interruptions can negatively affect their train of thought. Let the process flow and allow the interviewer to set the tone and pace of the interviewer. Trying to take control or interrupting will be off-putting and you run the risk of actually annoying the interviewer.

> **Key Fact**
>
> It's important to show you are in tune with the needs of the hiring manager. A good way to do this is to let them manage the interview. Give them the information they need when they need it and help them to make their decision.

Asking questions that are presumptuous or make you appear overly confident are definitely to be avoided. Anything that suggests you think you've already got the job is to be avoided. For example, it's not a good idea to talk about your holiday plans or travel commitments at the beginning of an interview. Let the interviewer do their job in deciding if you are the right fit or not. Do not distract them with extraneous or irrelevant information.

> **Key Fact**
>
> Every piece of information that you provide during the interview must convey your interest and suitability for the role. If something doesn't add value to your case, then don't bring it up.

If a question about your availability comes up, then that's the time to talk about your holiday or travel plans. You must respect the fact that the interviewer has to first decide whether they think you are a suitable candidate or not. Anything that interrupts or distracts the initial phase of the interview is to be avoided.

Good questions

When it's clear that the time for questions has arrived, you need to have some good questions ready.

> **Key Fact**
>
> **Good questions are ones that show that you've prepared well for the interview and are serious about the job.**

Top Preparation Tip:

It's a good idea to prepare some good open questions in advance of the interview. Some examples might include:

- Ask why the interviewer likes working for the business.
- Ask what's expected of the person who gets the job.
- Ask about career development and progression prospects.
- Ask what needs to be delivered in the role in order to be judged as successful.
- Ask about the main challenges in the role.
- Ask how the role fits in with the overall needs of the organisation.
- Ask about challenges that the hiring manage has and how you could help resolve them.

These are all good questions and show that you are thinking about the job and the business as a long-term career opportunity. You can ask about the interview process itself and when decisions will be made. People are often afraid to ask this. There's nothing wrong with trying to understand how the business manages its hiring process. It shows you're serious about the role and your job search.

Avoid poor questions

Inappropriate or badly timed questions can be quite off-putting for a decision maker. Asking about working hours and terms and conditions too early in the interview process can come across as presumptuous. It can suggest that self-interest is your main priority above all else. It certainly doesn't convey any interest in selling yourself. It won't help you convince the hiring manager that you will work hard to solve their problems and go a good job for them.

Don't ask questions that show you haven't done your research. A good challenging question that makes the interviewer stop and think always goes down well, if timed correctly. Good questions help demonstrate your interest and show a serious approach to job hunting. Don't ask questions for the sake of it. Sloppy or lazy questions don't reflect well on you. Asking lazy questions shows that you are happy to waste an interviewers time. Questions that could have been answered by some basic research before the interview should be avoided. They will only serve to annoy the hiring manager.

What if you don't have any questions?

Maybe you won't have any questions at the end of an interview. You could say that you're clear on everything from what's already been discussed. You can also say that you had questions prepared but they've all been answered already. Good candidates will always come prepared with a list of questions, literally written on a sheet of paper.

Top Preparation Tip:

> **I would advise bringing a list of questions with you. Take it out at the end of the interview and check if there's anything that hasn't already been discussed.**

This simple step shows a thorough level of preparation and also demonstrates that you are methodical in your approach.

Closing questions

When asking questions make sure you respect the fact that the interview is a competitive process. Make sure you respect the fact that the hiring manager is the final decision maker. Make sure to phrase your questions in a way that shows you respect their opinion and their final decision. You can ask if there's anything else they'd like to confirm or check before you finish. Don't beg for the job! Don't blurt out glib closing statements about working harder than anybody else. Don't make any statements that suggest desperation on your part. Thank the interviewer for their time. Tell them you've enjoyed meeting them and that you're very interested in working for them.

SUMMARY

- Everything you say and do must create a positive impression. Keep all your answers focused on selling your interest in the job and your ability to solve problems and get the job done.

- Always start the interview with a pre-planned positive comment or question.

- Always check that the interviewer is happy with your answers. Don't annoy them by failing to answer the questions they've asked.

- Let the interviewer manage the interview. Don't interrupt their process with badly timed questions.

- Prepare a list of good questions and bring it along with you.

- Always close the interview on a positive note.

SIN NUMBER FOUR

Creating The Fear That You Won't Fit In

The last thing any hiring manager wants to do is bring in somebody new who will upset existing team members. Not being a team player is a very common reason for candidate rejections. Let's look at some of the elements of how teams work. What makes any good team work well together? There are some key factors to consider:

Key Factors in Effective Teams

- All team members share similar objectives and have a common goal or target.
- Each team member plays to his or her strengths and understands the strengths of others in the team.
- Good teams always have open communication and honest feedback between members.
- There is always a positive climate in a good team with team members encouraging and supporting one another.
- Good team environments allow all team members to contribute. Everybody's contribution and opinion are valued.

We're all part of a team

Almost every job in the world requires interaction with other people and most of us are part of a team. Being able to work well with others and being a team player is very important to all hiring managers. You must be able to show that you can perform well in team environments. During an interview, the hiring manager is trying to form a judgement about what kind of team player you are. They will be considering all these factors when listening to your answers. They'll be searching for clues that show them how you interact with others when working in a team situation.

Having some good examples of things you've achieved as part of a team helps show you're a strong team player. It's good to show you understand how your contribution helps to achieve team goals. It shows you understand that the overall team goals can only be achieved if team members work well together.

> **Key Fact**
> It's important to demonstrate that you recognise the benefits of team work.

It's important to put team needs and goals ahead of your own individual needs or goals. **It's good to share examples of how teams you've worked in have been able to pull together and get the job done.** Maybe one team member was unable to contribute and the team pulled together to make sure the job got done.

Self-awareness

Self-awareness is a very useful skill to have and most successful people are very self-aware. They know their strengths and utilise them to their best ability. They also know their weaknesses and they take action to address them or they seek help from somebody better than themselves. Good teams always allow team members to do what they're best at. Team members compensate for each other's weaknesses.

A good team always makes best use of each individuals strengths. **Give some examples to demonstrate how you've combined team members strengths to deliver results.** Showing you are not afraid to seek help with tasks is also a good thing to share with an interviewer.

Feedback

Showing you can give and receive feedback is a key part of performing well in a strong team. Others need to feel confident that they can give you constructive criticism. This is vital to learning and improving performance – both for individuals and teams. **Think of some examples from previous jobs that show how you've learned from your manager or other team members.** Look at any successful people and they're always looking at ways to improve. They are always open to feedback or suggestions as to how they can improve results and performance.

Positive Climate

Every good team fosters a positive climate. Team members help and encourage one another. Any team member struggling with a problem will be able to rely on team mates to help them get things sorted. Showing that you can help create a positive environment helps foster a good impression of you as a team player. **You can demonstrate this by using examples of how you helped a team mate.** You can also talk about how a team mate helped you or encouraged you in some way.

Every opinion is valued

A good healthy team environment is one where everyone's input and opinion is valued. **Having examples to show that you work in this way gives a good indication that you're a team player.** A hiring manager is looking for you to show that you value help and feedback from colleagues. They want to see that you can give and take feedback from colleagues and respond in a positive way. They are keen to see that you are prepared to get stuck in and help colleagues if they are struggling. They want to see that you are prepared to ask for help from colleagues when you don't know what to do or are struggling yourself. They want to know you can be relied upon to help the team get the job done.

We can't all be friends!

What if you have had difficulties working with some people in the past? All of us, at some point, face difficulties working with other people. If this is the case, then you should show how you tackled the issue and worked together to find a solution. This can be a positive thing to bring up during an interview. It shows maturity and strong communication abilities and a willingness to solve problems. Being able to resolve personal difficulties and issues demonstrates good teamwork and leadership skills on your part.

Dealing with Problems

Hiring managers are always keen to get a sense of how you deal with difficulties or road-blocks. Problems are inevitable and being able to fix them is a valuable skill. All businesses value staff with a problem-solving mindset. You need to be able to show how you worked your way through any difficult issues with colleagues. Excessive or unnecessary conflict is not productive in a team environment. Working to avoid or at least minimise it is the correct response.

Make sure you can show that you can always work with people to resolve issues and avoid unnecessary conflict. Make sure you don't blame others when things have gone wrong. Bad things will always happen at some point – mistakes, delays, mix-up's, misunderstandings and errors are inevitable. How you deal with them, that's what an interviewer wants to understand. Any good response to an interview question about problems should always refer to understanding what happened. You need to show that you learned how to stop it happening again in future.

Top Preparation Tip:

- **Prepare some examples of team successes showing how team members combined strengths to get the job done.**
- **Show how you've helped team mates and also how you've learned from them.**

Working with difficult people

Personality clashes and difficult personalities can be quite common so we must all learn to work around them. Avoid talking about individuals or groups or other teams or functions in negative terms. It's important to show that you found a positive way to work around any tricky or challenging individuals or situations. Being a good team player means you can work with all the various types of personalities.

You must be able to show that you can be flexible and adaptable. Taking the time to get to know people and how they like to work is very important in teamwork situations. Having respect for the differences between team members is important to achieving a harmonious and productive work environment.

Why are you looking for a new job?

The question of why you're looking to leave your current role is very common. The interviewer will be looking to see how you'll describe your motivations for looking for a new role. There may be a fear that you left or are looking to leave because of difficulties in your job. People who don't get on well with others often turn out to be job hoppers. Any hiring manager will need to make sure that they are not hiring somebody who will bring problems into their team.

If you're not working right now, hiring managers will always want to understand the reasons why not. My advice is to be straight up and honest whatever the situation. You can actually turn the question to your advantage. You can use it as a way to explain why you're so keen on the role you're interviewing for. If you're bored in your current role for example. Here's your chance to explain why and to outline why the new role is more exciting or interesting to you.

It's important to avoid the temptation to be negative about your particular circumstances. You might hate your current job because of never ending pressure and constant overtime. You might not get on with your boss. Perhaps the job has become boring to you. Moaning about any of these things in the interview is not going to do you any favours. It creates the impression that you like to complain. Saying something like:

"while I initially enjoyed the challenge, the job has become repetitive. Of course, the work still has to be done but I'm finding it less challenging than I used to. That's the reason why I think it's time for a new challenge. I've learned a lot from the role and I'm ready now to do more."

Avoid Negativity

You must avoid talking negatively about your last or current job or boss. It's OK to outline why you want to leave but do so in positive language. Make sure to practice what you're going to say. Spend some time with a friend practicing how you explain your story. This is very important. All hiring managers will be very tuned in to the reasons why you are looking for a new job. They need to get it, and they need to get it quickly. No matter how complicated the situation make sure you can explain the key reasons.

> **Key Fact**
>
> You must always be able to explain clearly and simply the reasons why you are looking for a new role.

Never allow yourself to appear to be stubborn

It's important that you avoid saying anything which suggests that you are not easy to get along with. Awkward, stubborn or negative people can be very difficult to work with. These traits or behaviours have no place in a high performing team. A hiring manager will be put off by any suggestion that you don't react well to feedback or constructive criticism. Blaming others after the event rather than helping them when you can make a positive contribution is equally off-putting. Good team players will always want to share the credit with their colleagues. They won't hog the limelight.

Avoid office politics

Healthy, positive work environments will not be overly political. People are judged on their contribution and performance and not gossip, rumours or who they're friends with. It's best to avoid anything that suggests you might be the political type who enjoys gossiping about others. Some level of office politics is inevitable but its best to show that you rise above it in the workplace.

Make it relevant

Showing you can get along with people and are able to work well in team environments is very important. It's important to give some consideration to what's specifically expected in the role and refine your answers accordingly. Maybe the job you're interviewing for requires leadership skills. In that case, you will need to focus on your influencing and communication skills. You will need to prepare examples of these traits. Whether you will lead or are part of a team doesn't really matter. It's important to show the interviewer that you understand the benefits of team work. You must show that you appreciate how an effective team can solve problems and really get things done.

SUMMARY

- You need some examples that show how you work well in a team environment.

- You need to show you can get along with people and work together. Even when you're not the best of friends!

- You need to demonstrate that you can give and receive constructive feedback.

- You must avoid saying anything that suggests you are stubborn, argumentative or inflexible or that you look to blame others.

- You must be able to explain why you're looking for a new job.

- Never complain or make any negative comments about previous jobs, colleagues or managers.

- You must show that you understand the benefits of having a positive work environment. You must show that you will contribute in a positive way.

SIN NUMBER FIVE

Failing To Convince The Hiring Manager That You Want The Job

During any job interview, you can usually tell when you've convinced the interviewer that you meet the basic requirements. Once a hiring manager thinks you can do the job and will get on with existing staff their focus changes. It might be a subtle change but you will sense the tone changing from an interrogation to a conversation. If you hit this point then you know you're doing reasonably well. They've ticked two of the key boxes in their decision-making process.

Why do you want this job?

The next step is less about ensuring themselves you can do the work. It's much more focused on finding out if you want to do the work. If the hiring manager thinks you're a strong candidate the final step is making sure you'll enjoy doing the job. No manager likes to see good staff leave. It's particularly disruptive when a new team member doesn't work out. All managers are judged on their ability to hire and retain good staff. Losing new hires is particularly unfortunate and is to be avoided. They need to satisfy themselves that you will enjoy the work and will stay!

Think Long Term

As soon as you reach that point where the focus changes you need to change your tactics. You need to show that you have a real long-term interest in the business. You need to make it crystal clear that the job and the business will fulfill your expectations. Granted, there will be some uncertainty about the future and how things might work out. Despite that, you need to make a compelling argument as to why you'll want to stay working with the business. If you're already convinced of this now is your chance to show the hiring manager. Explain the main reasons why the job appeals to you. Explain why the business excites you and why it appeals in the long term. Good examples will explain why the industry or sector is exciting to you.

Career Development

It's a very good idea to ask about long term career development opportunities. You need to demonstrate that you've thought about sticking around if you do get offered the job. Asking questions about how to get promoted can be a good way of demonstrating your genuine interest. Asking what you would need to do to be promoted is a very good idea. It's important to show that you don't want any old job. Of course, you don't want to appear too pushy but mentioning your realistic ambitions is a good thing in an interview.

> **Key Fact**
>
> **A common reason for rejecting candidates is the fear that they will get bored or will be unhappy and will leave.**

You need to demonstrate that you've thought seriously about the prospect of actually getting the job. A good way of demonstrating that you are serious is by showing how you will apply your existing experience. You need to explain how your previous experience will bring advantages and benefits to this opportunity. It will help you to settle in and start adding value quickly.

You also need to show how and why you think the job will appeal to you on a personal basis. Perhaps it's a chance to step up in responsibility or to apply existing skills in a new sector or area. Learning new things might be exciting to you. Maybe the opportunity to meet and work with lots of new people appeals to you. Whatever the reason, the important thing is to tell the interviewer specifically why the role appeals to you. They must be convinced of the reasons why the job will be good for you.

Top Preparation Tip:

Identify the main reasons why the job appeals to you. Add them to your preparation checklist and be sure that you can explain them to the interviewer.

It's very important to show how you would apply yourself if you were to get the job. This is a common type of question you could be hit with. An interviewer may outline some current difficulties and will ask what would you do if you get the job. These can be tricky questions, so it's important to think about this situation before the interview. Doing your research will help. Having up to date and topical background information will go a long way towards impressing a decision maker.

You can refer to previous experience you may have had in similar situations. It's a good idea to have some examples ready, so you're not caught cold by this type of question. Better still you could ask the interviewer what current difficulties or challenges they face. This is a great way of showing that you're keen to understand their problems and how you would help solve them.

Show that you will be a valued team member

Always be positive and proactive in your approach. Show how your experience will help them. Making a positive impact and benefitting the business makes you a valued member of staff. Valued employees are the ones that get promoted and get the best career development opportunities. Show that you have the ambition to become a valued member of staff. This is the best way to convince a hiring manager that the job will be in your long-term interests.

Having the skills and attitude that are in line with business needs helps set you apart from other candidates. Knowing that you can do a good job reassures the hiring manager. It helps them see you as a potential valued team member if your expectations are aligned with business needs.

Show that you understand what they need

It's important to demonstrate that you understand the nature of the job. Showing that you don't is a big mistake. It's all well and good having the skills that meet the job specification but there's more to it than that. The company culture, the industry and challenges that the business faces will be important factors for the hiring manager to consider.

How will you fit in with the particular culture and challenges of the business? Have you made a convincing case that you will enjoy and thrive in their environment? Have you convinced the decision maker(s) that their organisation's difficulties and challenges are the type of problems you're good at fixing? Have you shown the interviewer(s) that you have the skills and personality to thrive in their organisation?

Are you the right type of person to fit in?

If it's not clear to you what type of people get on well in the business, then just ask. Ask what type of person is successful in their organisation. What skills or attributes are most highly valued by the business? Sometimes this isn't obvious to outsiders so there's no harm at all in asking an interviewer. Some things will be inherent to the role but certain skills and traits may be unique to the industry or the culture. Different managers will have different views or priorities. It's important that you understand what the hiring manager values in terms of key skills and attributes. If your strengths and interests align with their needs and challenges you have a good chance of getting the job. Clearly explaining why the job is aligned to your abilities and ambitions will help you to reassure the line manager.

Keep it real

It's always a good idea to show that you're looking to develop a long-term career with the employer. It's equally as important to be realistic and sensible with your ambitions. This is why it's a good idea to ask about existing staff and how they've progressed up through the ranks. If you march in announcing that you expect to be promoted to managing director within two years you may put the hiring manager off.

Unrealistic expectations will ultimately result in disappointment. The hiring manager needs to feel that your long term hopes and expectations are achievable within their business. They won't want to keep having to deal with disappointments and having discussions with you about lack of career progression. They'll need you to focus on the needs of the job. At the same time, they will need to know that there will be enough of a challenge to keep you interested and motivated.

SUMMARY

- You will, at some stage in the interview, need to convince the hiring manager that you want to do the job.

- Do not leave the interviewer in any doubt that you want the job and why you are excited about it.

- You need to demonstrate why the business has long term appeal for you.

- You need to demonstrate that you have the potential to become a highly valued employee. You need to show that you are the type of person they will want to promote, develop and retain.

- You will need to show that your ambitions and expectations are realistic.

- You need to demonstrate that your strengths and interests are aligned with the needs of the business.

SIN NUMBER SIX

Failing To Convince The Hiring Manager That They Will Want To Work With You

Managers are generally busy people. They usually have to balance a number of commitments and are nearly always time poor. They have to plan things, allocate work, check it's being done and report on what's been done. They have to deal with any issues or problems that come up. They have to make sure their team is performing and that each individual is performing. You will consistently notice that managers are nearly always short of time!

Good working relationships

To have a good working relationship with your boss, you must have a good understanding of what's expected of them. What are their objectives? What pressures are on them, what challenges do they face on a daily basis? So, what's this got to with the job interview? Well, during the interview you will need to convince any hiring manager that they will want to work with you. If you will be able to do what they ask then you're going to be a useful addition to their team. If they think that you are in tune with their needs and expectations then you will make it easier for them to manage you.

> **Key Fact**
>
> Hiring managers often reject candidates because they get the feeling that they will be difficult to work with.

Even with the right skills any hint of being difficult to manage will most likely put the hiring manager off. Very often this is one of the key reasons why hiring managers want references to be checked. They really want to know if there's a risk of problems arising.

When working with a manufacturing business to hire a new Operations Manager I saw a clear example of this need for good working relationships. The hiring manager was the Managing Director and he immediately rejected the candidate after the interview. "He had all the technical skills and was clearly an accomplished candidate. Despite this, I was put off because he showed very little respect for the people who worked for him. If he worked for us he would upset the people here and I just don't want to work with him." Having failed to build rapport with the hiring manager the candidate had created the fear that although he would get the job done he would upset people in the process. The Managing Director rejected him immediately for that reason. He just knew that he wouldn't have a good working relationship with the candidate.

Dealing with problems

With limited available time and resources available all managers are looking to build a team that's easy for them to manage. Difficulties in managing people takes up valuable time that could be spent on more productive things. There will always be a fear in any hiring managers mind that a candidate may be difficult to work with.

Your job is to convince the hiring manager that they will have no problems when managing you. You need to make it clear that it will be an easy and straightforward task for them. You need to convince them that you will make them look good and will help them do their job. You need to show that you can take constructive criticism. You need to show that you will get the job done and you will learn and improve with experience. If you can achieve these things then you are well on the way to making a very positive impression.

Put yourself in their shoes

You need to be able to put yourself in the shoes of the hiring manager. A very good way of doing this is demonstrating the good working relationships that you've had with previous managers. All managers like to be kept informed but don't necessarily need to know all the details. Managers generally want to know if there's a problem that's going to affect the results or the outcome of what should happen. They don't like unpleasant surprises. All managers like their team to be proactive, to anticipate problems and to come up with possible solutions. All managers like to get what they need when they need it. No manager likes to have to repeatedly ask or chase their staff for things.

Top Preparation Tip:

- **Prepare some examples that demonstrate how easy you are to manage.**
- **Prepare some examples that shows you are proactive in getting problems solved and getting things done on time.**
- **Prepare some examples that show that you take your responsibilities seriously and always meet your commitments.**

Add these examples to your preparation checklist.

You can demonstrate that you always come up with solutions and always have options to put on the table. You can show that you understand how important it is to keep your manager updated. You can demonstrate that you are always upfront and don't hide things, particularly bad news. At the same time, you'll show them that you won't come running with every little issue that crops up.

Working out the right style for your answers

As you progress through the interview, you'll get a sense of the working style of the interviewer. You'll get a sense of their style of communication. Do they like open ended discussions or are they more formal? You'll need to try and tailor your answers to their particular style. If they are very formal and like to stick to a rigid format then keep focused on short clear answers, stick to the facts. If they are more conversational then you should try to engage in more of an open conversational style. Offer your feelings and opinions, ask them questions, get some dialogue going. This is no different to how we deal with most people in our everyday lives. You just need to be tuned in to quickly learn what they like and dislike.

If the interviewer has to keep asking you for more details try to make your answers more specific and precise. If they seem impatient with wordy answers try to cut to the chase and only talk about outcomes and results.

Remember that you need to let them manage the interview in the way that they want. If you don't you run the risk of annoying them. This is not a clever tactic if you're trying to make a case that you will be easy to work with.

A key responsibility for all managers is decision making. To make effective decisions requires the right information. Not too much and not little. **Decision makers are looking for people who will give them the right information to make an informed, correct decision.** Answering their questions in a way that gives them what they need is crucial.

Key Fact

The interview itself is a key part of the hiring manager's decision-making process. It gives them a clear indication of how easy it will be for them to work with you.

You need to ensure that your style of answering questions shows you in a positive light. You need to be sure that you are helping the interviewer make a decision about your suitability for the job. Be sure to consider the following criteria as you formulate your answers and do your preparation prior to the interview:

Effective style of answers

- Are you answering the question that's been asked?

- Are you giving the interviewer what they need to know?

- Are you being evasive or avoiding specifics?

- Are you being positive and proactive with all your answers?

- Are you sense checking each answer and making sure the interviewer is happy with what you've said?

You must show that you can build a relationship and that you can be trusted to provide the information that's required. You need to be able to demonstrate that you can clearly explain things and allow a decision maker to get what they need from you. You must show that you are capable of having open and honest discussions. You must convey the fact that you are mature enough to accept decisions even if they go against you. To work effectively with any manager, you must be able to build a relationship, trust and respect.

Help them do their job

You must demonstrate that you will help the hiring manager to do their job. They need to feel comfortable that you will help them to look good. They absolutely need to get the sense that if they hire you, they will be able to trust you. It's very important that you show the hiring manager that they won't have to spend lots of time with you. It can be very demotivating for a manager if they have to spend excessive amounts of time with a team member. Nobody wants to be a micromanager especially if they have a large number of direct reports. You must show that you will be respectful of their time. They need to feel confident that you will deliver and get the job done for them with minimal supervision.

SUMMARY

- You must show that you understand the needs and objectives of the hiring manager.

- You must demonstrate that you will help them to do their job and help to make them look good.

- They must get the feeling that they can trust and rely upon you to get the job done.

- They need to feel confident that you will be able to give them the information that they need to make effective decisions.

- They need to know that you won't require lots of hand holding and won't take up too much of their time unnecessarily.

- They need to feel reassured that they will be able to build an effective, positive working relationship with you.

SIN NUMBER SEVEN

Showing That You Haven't Prepared For The Interview

Why is interview preparation so important? It's important to any hiring manager to see that you're serious about the role you're interviewing for. **If you make it obvious that you haven't prepared you're giving the interviewer a clear signal that you're not really that interested.** You are giving the impression that you're just making up the numbers and are not a serious candidate. Giving the impression that you're not too bothered and just looking for any old job won't help you.

Demonstrating to the interviewer that you've done some thorough research helps make a positive impression. It shows genuine interest and it shows you approach things in a professional manner. Being professional and well prepared is a key requirement in most business environments. Showing it during an interview helps build that strong positive impression of you as a professional candidate.

Good preparation will help you to relax and stay focused and calm during an interview. Difficult questions can throw you off course. Planning the key points that you want to make during the interview allows you to stay on track. This is especially true when the pressure comes on. Without effective preparation panic can set in when pressure is applied. Our brains can sometimes make us say things that we didn't intend to say when we're under pressure.

Key steps to being properly prepared

-   Identify the **key competencies** required for the job.

-   Know your **key strengths and abilities** and be ready to demonstrate them with **stories** and examples. Make sure you have supporting **evidence**.

-   Identify what the **hiring manager needs** and have examples prepared to show how you will meet their needs.

-   Do your **research** and be sure you can demonstrate that you understand the business and the culture.

-   Make sure you can explain why the job is of interest and why it **appeals to you**.

Add these key points to your interview preparation checklist

Awkward Silences

Awkward silences are uncomfortable. Without something to say most of us panic and start saying the first thing that comes into our heads. This is not a winning tactic in a job interview situation. You're under pressure, trying to impress somebody that you don't know. Having a plan in place helps to put your mind at ease and helps you to relax.

Effective preparation allows you to give structured answers and to make sure you get your key points across. It allows you to think and speak clearly, no matter how tough or challenging the questions. It's very disappointing to look back on an interview and realise afterwards that you neglected to bring up certain key points. The reality is an interviewer won't know what your key strengths are unless you do a good job of explaining them.

Key Fact

If you don't mention your key strengths and abilities how is the interviewer going to find out about them?

Interview questions

It's impossible to predict every type of interview question that might come up. Most interview questions relate to three general areas or topics.

Types of Interview Question

- Questions about your experience. Particularly how your experience might relate to the role you're interviewing for.

- Questions about the type of person that you are. The key focus will be on how you will fit in with existing staff and the culture of the organisation.

- If the interview is going well, you'll also face questions about your future expectations and aspirations.

Knowing about and planning for these three types of questions will help you to focus.

Top Preparation Tip:

- **Categorise your own key selling points and work them into your answers at the appropriate time.**
- **Prepare your answers in a way that will best show your abilities for each of the key required competencies or skills.**
- **Have some example stories ready that show the kind of person you are. Make sure these highlight your key strengths.**

Make sure that you highlight those traits and competencies that are most valued in the organisation and the role. In general hiring managers will be looking for examples that show you can get things done. They will also want to see evidence that you get on well with others when working in a team environment.

Anticipating the types
of questions you'll get

Anticipating the line of questioning that an interviewer will take helps you to look calm and well informed.

Try to think about and identify the key needs of the hiring manager. Add these to your preparation checklist.

If you can clearly explain how you meet those key requirements that shows you in a very positive light. All interviewers will be impressed by well researched answers. Being able to show that you understand their specific needs helps the hiring manager see you as a strong candidate. Showing that you have the key skills and attitude makes for a strong pitch to a hiring manager.

So how much do you need to know in order to be properly prepared? At the very least you need to make sure you know the basics details:

Basic details that you need to know

- Size and number of employees.
- Who are the main customers?
- Who are the main competitors?
- Are there any industry trends or new technologies or legislation changes that will affect the organisation?
- Any recent news, new contracts, awards won?
- What values and culture does the company promote? Check the company website for employee awards or quotes from senior staff.
- Look at the profiles of existing staff members on the professional networking sites. Do current staff have any common backgrounds, experience or qualifications?
- Check out the employer review websites to find staff comments and feedback about their employee experiences.
- Look out for general stories or articles about the organization.
- Talk to current and ex-employees.

Show you've done your homework

Arming yourself with this information allows you to show that you've been thorough in your research. It's a good tactic to drop pieces of information into any questions you will ask and the answers you provide. Do this deliberately to make it obvious that you know your stuff and that you've done your homework. This level of basic preparation will help you to stand out from other candidates. Your introduction when you first meet the interviewer is also a great opportunity to show you've done your research. Mentioning some recent news or other topical item can be a great conversation starter.

Don't forget that it's important to **show you've been researching the company. You've done the hard work so make sure you mention it during the interview.** You can ask strong questions by referring to your research. For example:

"From talking to current employees and doing some online research, I see you've grown a lot in recent years. Are there more growth plans in place?"

This a good open question that demonstrates you've done some homework and can form the basis of a good conversation.

Get the inside track

If you know, existing employees or people that work for customers or competitors make sure to talk with them. Don't forget about ex-employees, they're well worth talking to as well. You can easily find out who you might know by using any of the professional networking sites. If you don't know somebody directly, the chances are a friend of a friend or another contact of yours might know somebody. Get in touch and have a chat with them.

SUMMARY

- Good preparation helps you to look professional and creates a positive impression.

- Good preparation shows you are serious about your job search.

- Preparing some good answers and anticipating the interviewer's questions will help you to stay calm. This helps you to make sure you highlight all of your key selling points.

- Research the organisation and make sure you know the basic details.

- Make sure you show the interviewer that you've come prepared and have done your homework.

- Talk to current and previous employees.

CHAPTER EIGHT

Winning Habits, Behaviours And Tricks

So far, we've looked at the obvious pitfalls and how you can avoid them. **Avoiding failure is a key part of success but there's more to it than that.** There are a number of things that successful candidates consistently do in interviews. Some are simple tricks and tactics that help to remove fear from the hiring managers mind. Certain tactics help to create confidence and help them to build a clear picture of themselves as a strong candidate. Others are behaviours which are very appealing to all hiring managers.

Universal appeal

There are some general skills and behaviours which are pretty universally useful and highly valued in all organisations. For example, leadership, communication and problem-solving abilities are useful in all work scenarios. Showing that you have strengths in these areas will create a good impression. Winning candidates will knowingly drop these nuggets into the conversation without even being asked about them. Why wait for a question asking you to outline your leadership skills when you can casually drop them into the conversation? This type of trick really helps an interviewer – it allows them to tick the box without having to even ask you the question. So here are the key tactics, tricks and behaviours that successful candidates use to win over the hiring manager:

Show them that you want the job

Winning candidates always show that they really want the job. They are good at explaining how they'll be good at it. They will add value to the business because they'll be good at the job. They will really help their line manager to look good.

Show them you will fit in

Winning candidates explain how they will fit into the organisation. They are always convincing and show that they really understand what's required. They can always explain why the job will allow them to develop their careers. They can explain why the job will help them achieve their long-term aspirations. They show that they will be able to use their existing experience and apply it to the role.

If they don't have all of the necessary skills they will have a realistic plan to address any shortfall. They can explain how they will upskill themselves to the required level. They may even have already started working on it.

They will turn any skills gap into a potential selling point for themselves. They'll explain how upskilling in a certain area is very appealing to them.

Show them that you get things done

Successful candidates are always able to demonstrate that they get things done. They will always finish the job and deliver what's expected. They never have to be asked twice. They are also proactive and frequently do what's needed without having to be asked. They can demonstrate that they understand the needs of the business. This understanding is what helps them know what to do and when to do it.

Show them that you learn from your mistakes

Winning candidates don't have blind spots. They know they're not perfect and they can take feedback and constructive criticism. They will show that they welcome and encourage it. They will have lots of examples to show how they've learned from any past mistakes.

Answer the question that's been asked

Successful candidates always answer the question that's been asked. They always make sure they understand what the interviewer needs to know. If they're not sure, they ask questions to clarify what exactly the interviewer is looking for. They will also check and be sure that they've provided a satisfactory answer.

They will look for visual clues or any indications that shows they've given a good answer. If they suspect the interviewer is not happy or not sure about their answer, they will offer further information. They will do their best to make sure there's no doubt or confusion over their answers.

Be ready with some good questions

Successful candidates will always have some good questions prepared. They will be curious to understand the impact of the role they're interviewing for and how it affects the business. Their questions will always show their genuine interest in the organisation and the position. They will use their questions to make sure they are giving the interviewer all the information that they need.

Never assume anything

Successful candidates never make assumptions. They prepare thoroughly and they know what's required to do the job. If they are unsure about any of the requirements, they'll ask. They make sure they can explain why the role appeals to them.

Always listen carefully

Winning candidates always listen. They listen clearly and make sure to understand the questions that are being asked. They give the interviewer confidence that they will always get the job done and give their manager what they need.

Show that you are always in demand

Successful candidates will always find ways to show that others like working with them and that they are in demand. They will use examples which demonstrate how they've been asked to join teams and get involved in various projects. They will also mention that they have a number of avenues open to them as regards future career options.

Avoid the obvious pitfalls

Winning candidates always avoid the obvious pitfalls and always make a positive impression during the interview. They always demonstrate that they're good to work with and good to manage. They make it very clear to the hiring manager that they won't cause them problems and that they'll get the job done.

SUMMARY

The tricks, tactics, behaviors and techniques that are universally appealing to all hiring managers are summarized below:

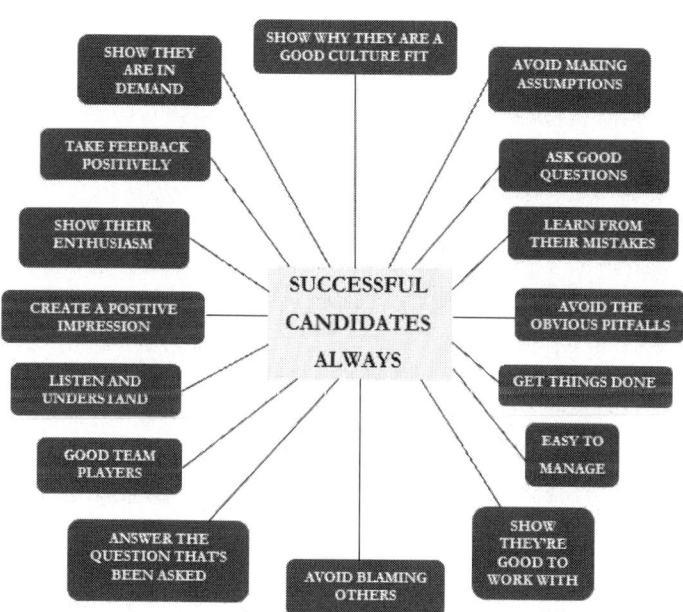

CHAPTER NINE

Reasons For Rejection And How You Can Avoid Them

Here we've summarised the most common reasons that cause interviewers to reject candidates. These have all been identified from direct hiring manager feedback.

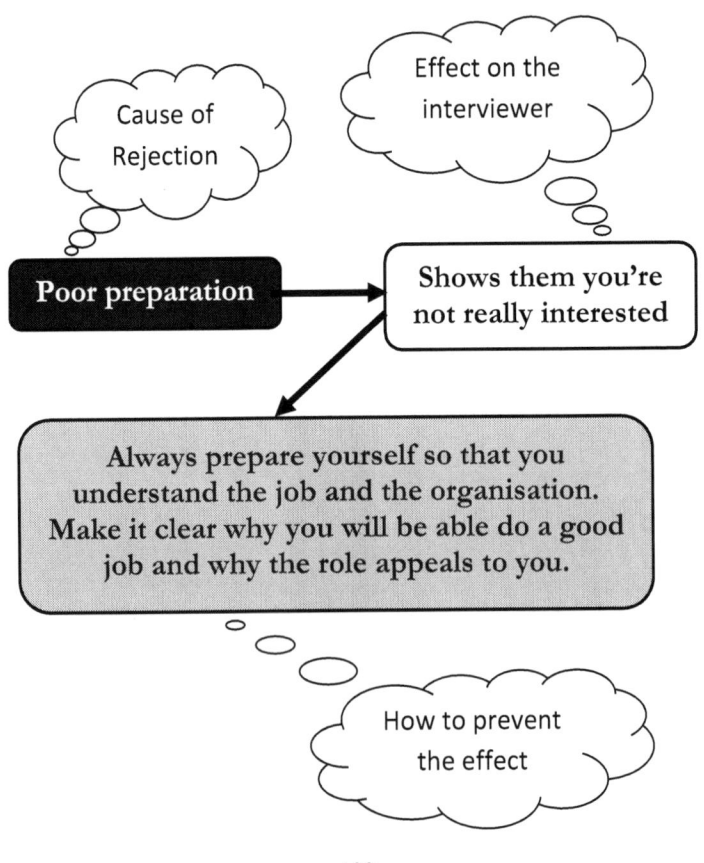

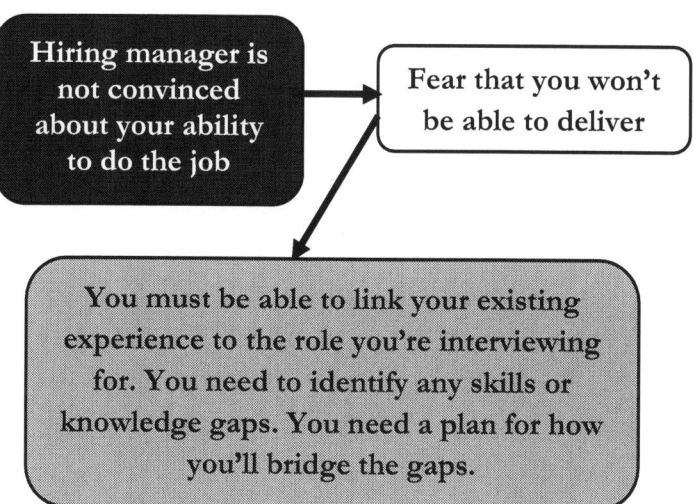

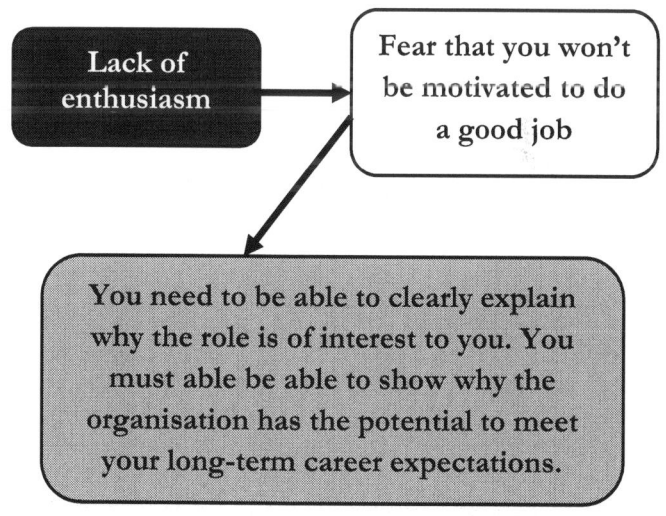

Giving the impression you're difficult to work with

Fear that you will cause problems and make their life difficult

You need to have some examples prepared that show other people ask for your help. You need examples that demonstrate you are a team player. You should explain how other people have asked you to get involved in projects and problem-solving activities.

Giving the impression that you can't get things done

Fear that they will have to spend lots of time chasing you to get things done

You need some examples that show you are prepared to take the initiative. You need to show that you are the type of person who will get things done. Make sure that you explain how you find ways around roadblocks or obstacles.

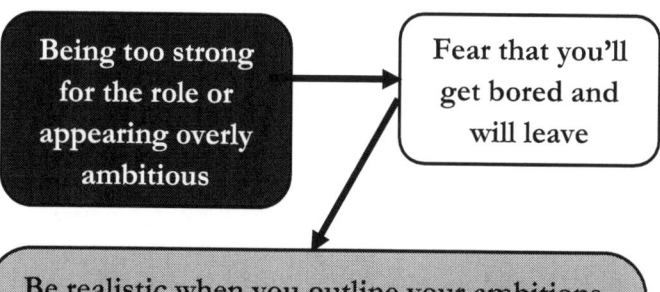

Being too strong for the role or appearing overly ambitious

Fear that you'll get bored and will leave

Be realistic when you outline your ambitions. Remember it takes two to three years to master most jobs. You should outline some reasons why the new role will allow you to learn new things and gain more experience.

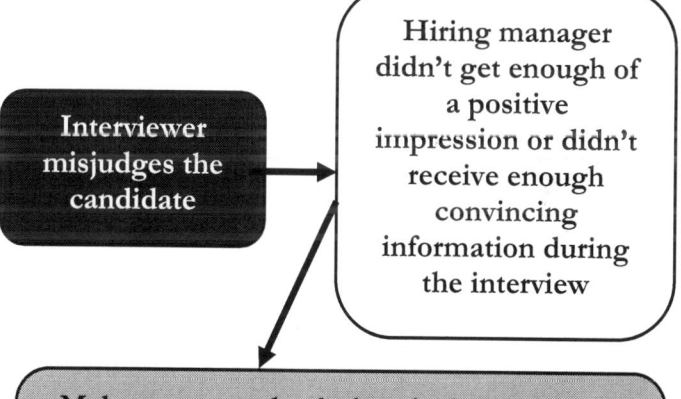

Interviewer misjudges the candidate

Hiring manager didn't get enough of a positive impression or didn't receive enough convincing information during the interview

Make sure you check that the interviewer is happy with your answers. If not make sure you offer more information. Never miss any opportunity to create a positive impression.

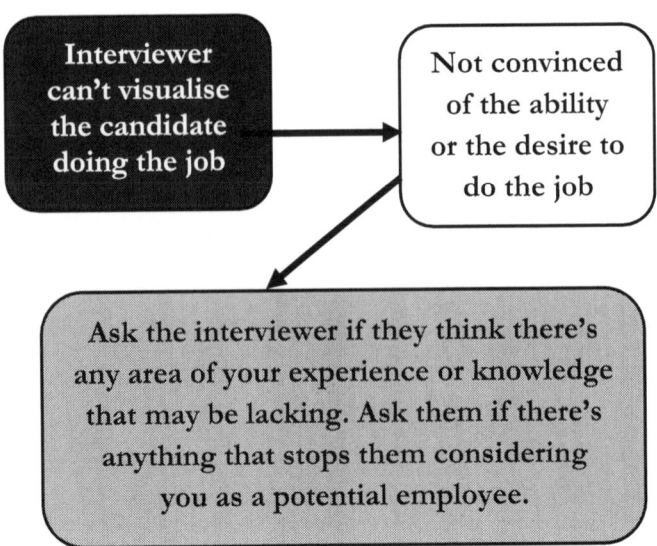

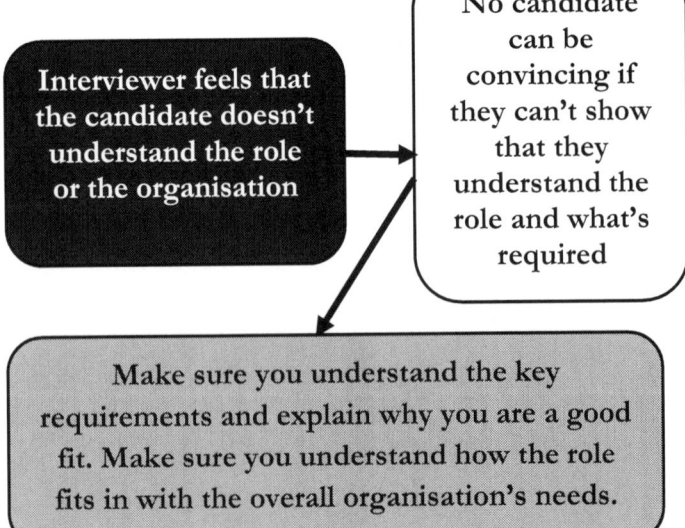

CHAPTER TEN

Job Interview Preparation Checklist

What are the key skills required?	Your rating? (1-5)
_____ _____ _____ _____	☐ ☐ ☐ ☐

How will you deal with any gaps in your skill level?

What do you think the hiring manager needs?

_____
_____
_____
_____
_____

What are your key strengths?

_____
_____
_____
_____
_____

Job Interview Preparation Checklist

Examples of how you learned something when things went wrong:

_____
_____
_____
_____

Examples of when you worked well with a team:

_____
_____
_____
_____

Examples of when you went "above and beyond" to get the job done or to solve a problem:

_____
_____
_____
_____

Examples of soft skills that you've used to good effect:

_____
_____
_____
_____

Job Interview Preparation Checklist

What is the Culture of the organisation?
Do current staff share any key characteristics?

What are the key values or attributes most valued by
the organisation?

_____

_____

_____

_____

What makes the job appealing to you?
Why is it better than your current role or employer?

Why are you the best candidate for the job?

Job Interview **Preparation** Checklist

Do you know the key details of the organisation?

Customers and Products or Services –

Size –
Ownership –
Competitors –
Markets –
Staff Reviews –
Recent news stories -

Have you prepared positive opening comments or questions?

Questions you need to ask at Interview:

---------- Thank you for reading this book. I hope you enjoyed it and that you found it useful. If you did then, please leave a Five Star Amazon review ---------

24416818R00066

Printed in Great Britain
by Amazon